BAKE
YOURSELF
Happy

BAKE YOURSELF HAPPY

First published in 2013
This edition copyright © Summersdale Publishers Ltd, 2015

Recipe research by Charlotte Williams, Abi McMahon

Summersdale Publishers Ltd
46 West Street
Chichester
West Sussex
PO19 1RP UK
www.summersdale.com

Printed and bound in the Czech Republic

ISBN: 978-1-84953-678-3

Substantial discounts on bulk quantities of Summersdale books are available to corporations, professional associations and other organisations. For details contact Nicky Douglas by telephone: +44 (0) 1243 756902, fax: +44 (0) 1243 786300 or email: nicky@ summersdale.com.

BAKE
YOURSELF
Happy

Cheering Food
For the Soul

EMMA HART

summersdale

CONTENTS

INTRODUCTION

From the soothing ritual of weighing, sifting and pouring to the stomach- and heart-stirring aromas that fill the house, baking can lift the gloomiest of souls and raise the heaviest of spirits. Whether you're creating the cheering cheesecake or the perky pie, you'll find it hard to keep that smile from your face. Soon you'll be sharing in both the fun and the food as you bake yourself and your loved ones happy!

TIPS FOR SUCCESSFUL BAKING

Use the best, freshest ingredients you can to ensure top-quality results.

For best results, use full-fat milk and butter.

To soften butter, leave it covered and out of the fridge for up to 1 hour. Any longer and it can spoil.

Eggs should be medium size.

Chilled eggs separate more easily than those at room temperature – so separate them first, and then leave to stand for 20–30 minutes to come to room temperature.

Read through the recipe first, making sure you have all the ingredients and equipment you will need, clean and to hand.

Preheat the oven fully to ensure even cooking.

Make sure all mixing bowls, pans, spoons and utensils are thoroughly cleaned, as oils or soap can affect the outcome of a recipe.

Use the correct size of baking tin or dish and measure all ingredients accurately.

Once a cake or bake mixture is ready, transfer it to the baking tin or dish and then into the preheated oven immediately. This is especially important if bicarbonate of soda is used in the recipe as it begins to react immediately.

Avoid opening the oven door during baking, as this can cause bakes to collapse.

Allow food to cool completely before storing it in airtight containers.

CAKES AND MUFFINS

FAIRIES AND BUTTERFLIES CAKES

Revisit your childhood with these little mouthfuls of sweetness and light. It's all about the sticky jam fingers and the buttercream all round your mouth.

Makes 10

Ingredients

For the buns:
110 g/4 oz caster sugar
110 g/4 oz butter
2 eggs
110 g/4 oz self-raising flour
½ tsp baking powder
1 tbsp milk

For the jam and buttercream filling:
50 g/2 oz butter

75 g/3 oz icing sugar
2 tbsp strawberry jam

Preparation method

Preheat the oven to 190 °C/375 °F/Gas 5. Line a 10 in. fairy cake tin with paper cases.

In a large bowl, beat together the sugar, butter and eggs until combined. Fold in the flour, add the baking powder and milk, and stir until smooth.

Half-fill each case with the mixture, and bake for 15–20 min.

Place on a wire rack and allow to cool completely.

For the buttercream, beat together the butter and icing sugar until smooth, leaving some icing sugar aside for dusting.

Using a sharp knife, cut a disc from the top of each cake, and cut each disc in half. Spread jam on top of each cake, then a spoonful of buttercream, and finish by arranging the two halves of the discs on the top to resemble butterfly wings. Use the leftover icing sugar to dust the tops.

FEEL LIKE A MILLIONAIRE SHORTBREAD

A vein of golden caramel lies between the chocolate and shortbread confection. Tap into it and enjoy good fortune and a rich taste with every mouthful.

Makes 9

Ingredients
....

For the shortbread:
175 g/6 oz butter
75 g/3 oz caster sugar
1 vanilla pod, seeds scraped out and kept
225 g/8 oz plain flour

For the caramel:
200 g/7 oz butter
400 g/14 oz condensed milk

4 tbsp golden syrup
1 tsp sea salt

For the topping:
340 g/12 oz milk chocolate

Preparation method

Preheat the oven to 180 °C/350 °F/Gas 4. Grease a 20 cm /8 in. square cake tin and line with baking paper.

In a large bowl, use your fingertips to rub together the butter, sugar and vanilla seeds. Sift in the flour and continue rubbing to form a rough dough.

Transfer to the cake tin and press down to compact. Bake for 40 min, reducing the heat of the oven to 150 °C/300 °F /Gas 2 after 10 min. Allow to cool in the tin.

In a large saucepan, bring the butter, condensed milk, syrup and salt to the boil and simmer for 10 min. Pour the mixture over the shortbread, then chill in the fridge for 30 min until hardened.

Gently melt the chocolate in a heatproof bowl over a pan of boiling water. Pour the chocolate over the caramel and chill in the fridge for a further 30 min, or until set. Cut into squares.

ROCKIN' CAKES

Had a hard day facing the music? Get your groove back with these handfuls of sugar, sultanas and cake.

Makes 8

Ingredients

....

225 g/8 oz self-raising flour
½ tsp ground mixed spice
½ tsp ground cinnamon
110 g/4 oz butter
110 g/4 oz demerara sugar
50 g/2 oz sultanas
50 g/2 oz currants
1 egg, beaten
1 tbsp milk

Preparation method

Preheat the oven to 180 °C/350 °F/Gas 4. Line a baking tray with baking paper.

In a large bowl, sift the flour and add the mixed spice and cinnamon. Rub in the butter using your fingertips, then add the sugar, currants and sultanas and mix well.

Add the egg and combine to form a dough. Add a splash of milk if necessary.

Use a wooden spoon to place large dollops of the dough on the baking tray, then sprinkle with sugar.

Bake for 10–12 min, or until golden brown.

Where there is cake,
there is hope. And there
is always cake.

DEAN KOONTZ

A compromise is the art of dividing a cake in such a way that everyone believes he has the biggest piece.

LUDWIG ERHARD

CHELSEA FUNS

Sometimes when there's no fun to be had, you just have to make your own. Make a batch of these currant buns and have fun enough to spare!

Makes 6

Ingredients

....

For the bread:
250 g/9 oz white bread flour
2 tsp caster sugar
7 g/¼ oz dried active yeast
120 ml/4 fl oz warm milk
25 g/1 oz butter

For the filling:
50 g/2 oz dark brown sugar
50 g/2 oz butter, cubed
50 g/2 oz currants
50 g/2 oz sultanas
25 g/1 oz cut mixed peel

For the glaze:
2 tbsp milk

Preparation method

In a large bowl, beat together 75 g/3 oz of the flour, the sugar, yeast and warm milk until combined.

Allow to stand for 30 min.

In a separate bowl, rub together the butter and remaining flour to resemble breadcrumbs. Transfer to the first mixture, which should now be frothy, and fold together, then knead to form a smooth dough.

Lay a damp tea towel over the bowl and leave to stand for 1 hr.

Knead well. On a lightly floured work surface, roll out the dough to a 1 cm/½ in. thickness, in a rectangle.

Scatter half of the brown sugar evenly over the dough, then scatter the butter cubes, currants, sultanas and peel over, and top with the remaining sugar. Roll the dough lengthways to form a Swiss roll.

Line a large baking tray with baking paper. Using a sharp knife, cut into six pieces lengthways, and place them, spaced well apart, cut-side down on the tray. Cover again with a damp tea towel and leave to stand for 40 min.

Meanwhile, preheat the oven to 200 °C/400 °F/Gas 6. Brush the buns with a little milk, then bake for 30 min, or until golden brown.

*Seize the moment.
Remember all those women
on the Titanic who waved
off the dessert cart.*

ERMA BOMBECK

CHOCOLATE CELEBRATION CAKE

Celebrate life, love and happiness, or even cake itself. Made using only the tastiest, cheeriest ingredients, this is a party in your mouth and you are invited!

Serves 8–10

Ingredients

....

For the cake:
150 g/5 oz butter
275 g/10 oz dark brown sugar
3 eggs, beaten
225 g/8 oz plain flour
50 g/2 oz cocoa powder
2 tsp baking powder
½ tsp bicarbonate of soda
225 ml/8 fl oz milk
2 tsp vanilla extract

For the chocolate icing:
200 g/7 oz plain chocolate
200 ml/7 fl oz double cream

Preparation method

Preheat the oven to 180 °C/350 °F/Gas 4. Grease two 20c m/8 in. round sandwich tins and line with baking paper.

In a large bowl, beat together the butter and sugar, then gradually add the eggs. Sift in the flour, cocoa powder, baking powder and bicarbonate of soda and fold to combine. Slowly add the milk and vanilla extract, stirring continuously.

Pour half of the mixture into each tin, and bake for 30 min. Remove from the oven and allow to cool completely.

Meanwhile, heat the chocolate and cream in a small pan over a low heat until the chocolate is melted, then remove from the heat. Whisk together until smooth and thick. Leave to cool and thicken for 1 hr.

Remove the cakes from their tins. Spread chocolate icing over one cake, then place the other cake on top. Spread the remaining icing over the whole cake with a palette knife.

Blessed be he that invented
the pudding – to come in
pudding time is to come to
the most lucky moment
in the world.

FRANCIS MAXIMILIAN MISSON

*Let's face it, a nice creamy
chocolate cake does a lot for
a lot of people; it does for me.*

AUDREY HEPBURN

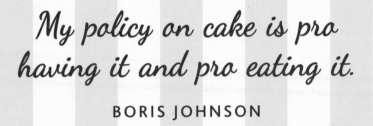

*My policy on cake is pro
having it and pro eating it.*

BORIS JOHNSON

SUNSHINE AFTER THE DRIZZLE CAKE

The tart, lemony drizzle on this cake means you'll have a slice of summer and sunshine on your plate, whatever the weather!

Serves 8–10

Ingredients

For the cake mixture:
225 g/8 oz butter
225 g/8 oz caster sugar
grated zest of 2 lemons
4 eggs, beaten
1 tsp baking powder
225 g/8 oz self-raising flour

For the icing:
Juice of 2 lemons
110 g/4 oz icing sugar

Preparation method

Preheat the oven to 180 °C/350 °F/Gas 4. Grease a 20 cm/ 8 in. round cake tin and line with baking paper.

In a large bowl, beat together the butter and sugar until light and fluffy. Add the lemon zest, eggs and baking powder, stirring well, then sift in the flour and fold until well combined.

Transfer the mixture to the cake tin and bake for 1hr 15 min.

While the cake is cooling in its tin, mix together the lemon juice and icing sugar. Using a skewer or fork, prick the warm cake all over, then pour over the lemon and sugar mix.

Leave the cake in the tin until completely cool before removing from the tin and serving.

FINEST MARBLE CAKE

Don your silk pyjamas, lounge upon your chaise longue and enjoy this delicacy, made with the richest cocoa and luxurious vanilla extract. This chocolate and vanilla artwork will make you feel rich in life, if not in purse.

Serves 6–8

Ingredients

225 g/8 oz butter
225 g/8 oz caster sugar
4 eggs, beaten
225 g/8 oz self-raising flour
3 tbsp milk
1 tsp vanilla extract
2 tbsp cocoa powder

Preparation method

Preheat the oven to 180 °C/350 °F/Gas 4. Grease a 20 cm/8 in. cake tin and line with baking paper.

In a large bowl, beat together the butter and sugar, then gradually add the eggs, stirring continuously. Sift in the flour and fold into the mixture, then stir in the milk.

Pour half of the mixture into a separate bowl, and add the cocoa powder to one half and the vanilla extract to the other, stirring well.

Alternate spoonfuls of each mixture into the cake tin, then use a skewer to swirl the mixture around within the tin to marble.

Bake for 50 min.

BRILLIANCE PIES

Though Christmas only comes once a year, mince pies are so brilliant they should be baked whenever possible. They're a little pastry cup of cheer!

Makes 12–16

Ingredients

....

225 g/8 oz plain flour
150 g/5 oz butter, diced
50 g/2 oz caster sugar
grated zest of 1 orange
pinch of salt
1 egg yolk
2 tsp water
275 g/10 oz mincemeat
1 egg, beaten
2 tbsp icing sugar

Preparation method

Preheat the oven to 200 °C/400 °F/Gas 6. Grease a 12–16-hole tart tray.

In a large bowl, using your fingertips, rub together the flour, butter and sugar. Add the orange zest and salt and stir well. Add the egg yolk and water and stir until combined. Wrap in cling film and chill in the fridge for 30 min.

On a lightly floured work surface, gently roll the pastry out to 2 mm/$\frac{1}{10}$ in. thick, and cut into rounds to slightly overfill the holes in the tray. Press one round into each hole.

Place a few spoonfuls of mincemeat into the centre of each pie, and form lids from the leftover pastry using shaped pastry cutters. Brush the tops with the beaten egg.

Bake for 12–15 min. Place on a wire rack and allow to cool, then dust with icing sugar.

SCRUMPY PUMPY CAKE

Take a hearty breath of fresh air with this cider cake straight from the soul of the West Country. Crammed with big jolly handfuls of nuts and sultanas, and spiced and sugared, it will put the colour back in your cheeks.

Serves 6–8

Ingredients

350 ml/12 fl oz cider
150 g/5 oz dark brown sugar
150 g/5 oz butter
4 cooking apples, peeled and grated
2 eggs, beaten
300 g/11 oz plain flour
2 tsp baking soda
1 tsp mixed spice
1 tsp ground cinnamon

pinch of freshly grated nutmeg
200 g/7 oz golden sultanas
110 g/4 oz chopped pecans

Preparation method

Preheat the oven to 180 °C/350 °F/Gas 4.

Grease a 20 cm/8 in. easy-release or springform cake tin.

Boil the cider in a small pan over a medium heat until reduced by two thirds.

In a large bowl, beat together the sugar and butter until light and fluffy. Add the grated apple, eggs and cider, and stir well.

In a separate bowl, sift the flour and add the baking soda, mixed spice, cinnamon and nutmeg. Stir well, then pour in the cider and apple mixture. Fold in the sultanas and pecans, and stir.

Transfer to the cake tin and bake for 50–60 min.

VICTORIA SPONGE

When you're feeling weak and feeble, get the stomach of a queen with a slice of this classic sponge, beloved by royalty and the WI across the land.

Serves 10–12

Ingredients

For the cake:
225 g/8 oz butter
225 g/8 oz caster sugar
4 eggs
2 tsp vanilla extract
225 g/8 oz self-raising flour
1 tbsp milk

For the filling:
jam and/or whipped cream

To serve:
caster sugar

Preparation method

Preheat the oven to 180 °C/350 °F/Gas 4. Grease two 18 cm/7 in. cake tins and line with baking paper.

Beat the butter and the sugar in a bowl until they are light and fluffy. Beat in the eggs and vanilla extract.

Fold in the flour, adding milk if needed, to make the batter.

Divide the mixture between the cake tins and use a spatula to create a smooth surface.

Bake for 20–25 min, or until golden brown.

Remove from the oven and leave to stand for 5 min. Remove from the tin and peel off the paper, placing the cakes on a wire rack to cool completely.

Spread jam or whipped cream (or both!) onto the top of one of the cakes, and then place the second on top to form a sandwich. Dust with caster sugar.

WELSH HARVEST CAKE

This cake spilleth over with apples and currents, and is a welcome reviver for your strength and spirits.

Serves 10–12

Ingredients

. . . .

175 g/6 oz butter
175 g/6 oz brown sugar
2 eggs, beaten
225 g/8 oz self-raising flour
½ tsp mixed spice
½ tsp ground cinnamon
450 g/1 lb cooking apples, peeled, cored and diced
50 g/2 oz sultanas
50 g/2 oz currants
50 g/2 oz flaked almonds

Preparation method

Preheat the oven to 180 °C/350 °F/Gas 4. Grease an 18 cm/7 in. cake tin and line with baking paper.

In a small pan, gently melt the butter and sugar, then remove from the heat. Add the eggs and beat to combine.

In a large bowl, sift the flour, mixed spice and cinnamon, then pour in the melted butter mix. Stir well.

In a separate bowl, mix the apples, sultanas, currants and almonds together.

Transfer half the mixture into the cake tin. Pour the fruit mix on top, and then top with the remaining cake mixture.

Bake for 55–60 min. Place on a wire rack and allow to cool completely.

APPLE TURN UP FOR THE BOOKS

Bake yourself these light pastry confections and save one for tomorrow, to give yourself a sweet surprise after a gloomy day.

Serves 4

Ingredients

....

25 g/1 oz butter
50 g/2 oz brown sugar
1 cooking apple, peeled, cored and sliced
25 g/1 oz raisins
½ tsp ground cinnamon
4 sheets ready-made filo pastry
1 egg, beaten

Preparation method

Preheat the oven to 220 °C/425 °F/Gas 7. Lightly grease a large baking tray.

Gently heat the butter and sugar in a small pan, then add the apple, raisins and cinnamon, and stir well. Remove from the heat when the sugar is dissolved and the apples begin to soften.

Lay out each sheet of pastry and cut into four smaller squares. Place them on the baking tray, then spoon some of the apple mixture into the centre of each square.

Brush the edges with the beaten egg, fold over one corner to create a triangle and press the sides together firmly to seal.

Brush the tops of the turnovers with beaten egg.

Bake for 10 min.

BAKE-YOURSELF-WELL TART

Cut yourself a slice of summer and brighten your spirits with this sweet, jammy tart.

Serves 8

Ingredients

....

For the pastry:
110 g/4 oz plain flour
75 g/3 oz butter, diced
25 g/1 oz caster sugar
pinch of salt
1 egg yolk
1 tbsp cold water

For the filling:
150 g/5 oz butter
150 g/5 oz caster sugar

3 eggs, beaten
1 egg yolk
grated zest of 1 lemon
150 g/5 oz ground almonds
2 tbsp raspberry jam
1 tbsp flaked almonds

Preparation method

In a large bowl, sift the flour and add the butter, sugar
and a pinch of salt, and combine. Add the egg yolk and
the water, and mix well to form a dough.

Gently flatten the dough into a disc shape, cover with
cling film and chill in the fridge for 1 hr.

On a lightly floured work surface, roll out the pastry thin
enough to line a 20 cm/8 in. fluted tart tin, then chill in
the fridge for 20 min.

Preheat the oven to 180 °C/350 °F/Gas 4.

Line the tin with the pastry, then line the pastry with baking paper. Fill with baking beans, and blind bake for 20 min, or until light brown. Remove from the oven and allow to cool for 5 min.

In a bowl, beat the butter and sugar until combined, then add the eggs and egg yolk, lemon zest and ground almonds.

Spread jam on the base of the tart, then pour in the filling mix. Use a spatula to smooth the top.

Bake for 35–40 min, until golden brown, sprinkling the flaked almonds on top halfway through cooking.

If 3.14 equals pi,
then what is cake?

CAROLYN YANG

GO BANANAS BREAD

Is your week driving you round the twist? Then go bananas with this delicious and filling sweet bread.

Serves 12

Ingredients

110 g/4 oz butter
225 g/8 oz caster sugar
2 eggs, beaten
4 small ripe bananas, mashed
90 ml/3 fl oz milk
1 tsp vanilla extract
275 g/10 oz plain flour
1 tsp bicarbonate of soda

Preparation method

Preheat the oven to 180 °C/350 °F/Gas 4. Grease a 20 cm x 12.5 cm/8 in. x 5 in loaf tin.

In a large mixing bowl, beat together the butter and sugar until light and fluffy. Add the eggs, bananas, milk and vanilla extract, and stir well.

Sift in the flour and bicarbonate of soda and fold the mixture until combined.

Transfer the mixture to the loaf tin and bake for 55–60 min, or until golden brown.

BATTEN DOWN THE HATCHES CAKE

When life's storms are stirring, close the windows, batten down the hatches and indulge in this light, bright confection.

Serves 6

Ingredients

....

150 g/5 oz butter
150 g/5 oz caster sugar
3 eggs, beaten
1 vanilla pod, seeds scraped out and kept
30 ml/1 fl oz milk
150 g/5 oz self-raising flour
1 tsp pink food colouring
75 g/3 oz apricot jam
200 g/7 oz ready-rolled marzipan

Preparation method

Preheat the oven to 200 °C/400 °F/Gas 6. Grease a 15 cm/6 in. square cake tin.

In a large bowl, beat the butter, sugar, eggs, vanilla seeds and milk together. Gradually sift in the flour and continue to beat until smooth.

Divide the mixture equally between two bowls, and add the food colouring to one bowl of mixture, stirring well.

Fold a square of aluminium foil so that it creates a division lengthways down the middle of the cake tin, and covers the bottom. Transfer the plain cake mixture to one side of the tin and the pink cake mixture to the other.

Bake for 30 min. Place on a wire rack, remove foil and allow to cool.

Cut both cakes in half lengthways. Take one yellow piece of cake and spread one side with jam, then place one pink piece next to it and press them together. Repeat with the remaining pieces. Spread a layer of jam on top of the two pieces of cake, then place the remaining combined pieces of cake on top, pink on yellow and yellow on pink. Spread jam all over the top and sides of the cake.

Cut the marzipan so that it's slightly longer than the cake, then wrap it round the sides of the cake, pressing gently so that it sticks to the jam. Turn the cake upside down and use a little jam to seal the edges together. Place seal-side down on a serving plate, and chill in the fridge for 30 min to set.

Never spare the Parson's wine, nor Baker's Pudding.

BENJAMIN FRANKLIN

FINE 'N' DANDY SNAPS

Munch on these ginger biscuits and, quick as a snap, everything will be dandy again!

Makes 12

Ingredients

....

110 g/4 oz butter
110 g/4 oz caster sugar
4 tbsp golden syrup
juice of ½ a lemon
110 g/4 oz plain flour
1 tsp ground ginger

Preparation method

Preheat the oven to 180 °C/350 °F/Gas 4. Use baking paper to line a large baking tray.

Gently heat the butter, sugar and syrup in a small pan until melted.

Remove from the heat and add the lemon juice. Sift in the flour and ginger. Stir well, and allow to cool.

Use a tablespoon to drop the mixture onto the baking tray, spaced well apart from each other (about 10cm/ 4 in.).

Bake for 5–7 min.

Working as quickly as possible, take each dandy snap, one at a time, and wrap it gently around the handle of a wooden spoon to form a coil shape.

Slide the dandy snap off the handle as soon as it hardens and leave to set.

DESSERTS

SIMPLE PLEASURES
BREAD AND BUTTER
PUDDING

Some days all you need to feel good are your comfy clothes and a big bowl of something lovely – this quick and easy pudding.

Serves 4

Ingredients

....

25 g/1 oz butter
8 slices of white bread
50 g/2 oz sultanas
2 tsp ground cinnamon
2 eggs
25 g/1 oz caster sugar
350 ml/12 fl oz milk
60 ml/2 fl oz double cream

1 tbsp demerara sugar
1 tsp freshly grated nutmeg

Preparation method

Grease a 1 litre/35 fl oz ovenproof dish.

Spread butter on each slice of bread, cut off the crusts, and cut into triangles.

Place a layer of the bread in the dish, topped with a layer of sultanas and a sprinkling of cinnamon. Repeat this layering process until you have used up all the bread.

In a bowl, crack the eggs and add the caster sugar, then whisk until combined.

Gently warm the milk over a low heat and pour into the bowl. Add the cream and stir well to form a custard. Strain if necessary.

Transfer the custard onto the bread pudding, and top with the demerara sugar and the nutmeg. Leave to stand for 30 min.

Preheat the oven to 180 °C/350 °F/Gas 4.

Place the dish in a roasting pan and fill the roasting pan halfway up with boiling water. Bake for 35 min, or until golden brown.

CHOCOLATE FUDGE PUDDLE PUDDING

When it's cold and rainy outside pull up your boots and go jumping in puddles; then dry off with towels and splash around in the pools of chocolate with this pudding.

Serves 4

Ingredients

....

For the sponge:
75 g/3 oz self-raising flour
25 g/1 oz cocoa powder
pinch of salt
110 g/4 oz muscovado sugar
110 g/4 oz butter
1 tsp vanilla extract
2 eggs, beaten
2–3 tbsp milk

For the sauce:
75 g/3 oz muscovado sugar
25 g/1 oz cocoa powder
200 ml/7 fl oz milk

Preparation method
....

Preheat the oven to 180 °C/350 °F/Gas 4. Grease a
1 litre/35 fl oz ovenproof dish.

In a large bowl, sift the flour and add the cocoa powder
and salt.

In a separate bowl, beat the sugar, butter and vanilla
extract together until light and fluffy, then gradually add
the eggs. Pour this mixture into the first bowl, and fold
to combine, adding just enough milk so that the mixture
drops easily off the spoon.

For the sauce, mix the sugar and cocoa powder in a
small bowl and add the milk, beating until smooth.

Transfer the sponge mixture into the ovenproof dish, then
pour the sauce on top.

Bake for 45–60 min.

CLOUDY SUNRISE PIE

Sharp as a fresh spring morning, with soft clouds of meringue curling around your tongue, this is the perfect way to wake your senses.

Serves 6–8

Ingredients

For the pastry:
225 g/8 oz plain flour
pinch of salt
110 g/4 oz butter, diced
2 tsp caster sugar
1 egg yolk
1 tsp water

For the lemon curd:
110 g/4 oz caster sugar

7 tbsp cornflour
60 ml/2 fl oz water
grated zest and juice of 4 lemons
6 egg yolks
110 g/4 oz butter, melted

For the meringue:
6 egg whites
300 g/11 oz caster sugar

Preparation method

In a large bowl, sift the flour and add the salt and butter. Rub together using your fingertips until the mixture resembles breadcrumbs.

Add the sugar and egg yolk, and mix, adding a splash of water if necessary, to form a dough.

Wrap the dough in cling film and chill in the fridge for 30 min.

Preheat the oven to 190 °C/375 °F/Gas 5. Grease a 23 cm/ 9 in. tart tin.

On a lightly floured work surface, gently roll out the pastry thin enough to line the tin, with excess pastry over the sides.

Line the pastry with baking paper, fill with baking beans and blind bake for 15 min.

Remove the baking paper and beans, and return to the oven for a further 5 min, or until golden brown.

Reduce the heat of the oven to 150 °C/300 °F/Gas 2. Tidy the edges of the pastry using a sharp knife.

In a large bowl, mix the sugar and cornflour with enough water so that it forms a paste.

Gently heat the rest of the water with the lemon zest in a small pan until it comes to the boil, then pour into the bowl and whisk to combine. Beat in the lemon juice, egg yolks and butter. Pour back into the pan.

Heat gently until the mixture thickens, then pour into the pastry case and leave to stand for 5 min.

In a large bowl, whisk the egg whites vigorously until they form peaks, then gradually add the sugar, whisking all the time. Transfer the meringue onto the lemon curd, and bake for 40 min.

Oh, a wonderful pudding!
Bob Cratchit said, and calmly
too, that he regarded it as
the greatest success achieved
by Mrs Cratchit since
their marriage.

CHARLES DICKENS

NEVER MIND THE COBBLERS

Sometimes the only solution for a load of cobblers is more cobblers! Only this cobbler is packed with plums, pears, sugar, nutmeg and cinnamon, and leaves a good taste in your mouth.

Serves 4–6

Ingredients

....

For the filling:
450 g/1 lb plums, stoned and quartered
450 g/1 lb pears, peeled, cored and sliced
75 g/3 oz muscovado sugar
½ tsp freshly grated nutmeg
½ tsp ground cinnamon

For the topping:
50 g/2 oz butter
225 g/8 oz self-raising flour
25 g/1 oz caster sugar
90 ml/3 fl oz milk

Preparation method

Preheat the oven to 200 °C/400 °F/Gas 6.

Gently simmer the plums, pears, sugar, nutmeg and cinnamon in a small pan over a low heat until the pears soften. Transfer to an ovenproof dish.

In a large bowl, beat together the butter and flour. Gradually add the sugar and milk, stirring well to form a dough.

On a lightly floured work surface, roll out the dough to a 1 cm/½ in. thickness, and cut into rounds.

Place the rounds on top of the pear and plum filling and brush with milk.

Bake for 20 min, or until golden brown.

SWEETNESS AND LIGHT PUDDING

Let your troubles float away in a puff of pudding and your cares melt on your tongue as you eat this simply dreamy dessert.

Serves 4

Ingredients

....

75 g/3 oz caster sugar
2 eggs, separated
25 g/1 oz self-raising flour
50 g/2 oz butter
300 ml/10 fl oz milk
pinch of salt

Preparation method

Preheat the oven to 180 °C/350 °F/Gas 4. Grease a 15 cm/6 in. ovenproof dish.

In a large bowl, beat together the sugar, egg yolks, flour, butter, milk and salt to form a batter.

Whisk the egg whites until they form stiff peaks, then gradually fold into the mixture.

Transfer to the ovenproof dish, place the dish inside a large roasting tray and fill the tray with boiling water.

Bake for 40 min, or until light golden brown.

SPOTTED DICK

If the name of this pudding doesn't make you laugh yourself happy then the taste surely will! Delicious served with custard (sunshine sauce).

Serves 6–8

Ingredients

300 g/11 oz plain flour
2 tsp baking powder
150 g/5 oz shredded suet
75 g/3 oz caster sugar
110 g/4 oz currants
grated zest of 1 lemon
200 ml/7 fl oz milk

Preparation method

In a large bowl, sift the flour and add the baking powder, suet, sugar, currants and lemon zest, and mix well.

Gradually add the milk, stirring well to form a dough.

Grease a pudding basin. Transfer the dough into the basin and cover with baking paper. Tie a piece of string around the edge to hold the paper in place, then place a damp tea towel on top and tie again to secure it in place.

Place the pudding basin in a large saucepan, filling two thirds with cold water. Cover, bring to the boil and simmer for 1 hr, checking periodically to ensure it hasn't boiled dry.

TOPPING STICKY TOFFEE PUDDING

When you're having a jolly rotten day you need an utterly spiffing pudding to pick you up by the socks, what! This top-hole pudding is just the ticket.

Serves 4

Ingredients

For the sponge:
300 ml/10 fl oz tea, freshly made and still hot
225 g/8 oz dates, chopped
110 g/4 oz butter
175 g/6 oz demerara sugar
3 eggs, beaten
225 g/8 oz self-raising flour
1 tsp bicarbonate of soda
1 tsp vanilla extract

For the sauce:
110 g/4 oz butter
175 g/6 oz demerara sugar
110 g/4 oz caster sugar
275 g/10 oz golden syrup
225 ml/8 fl oz double cream
1 tsp vanilla essence

Preparation method

Preheat the oven to 180 °C/350 °F/Gas 4. Grease an ovenproof dish.

Pour the tea into a large bowl, then add the dates, and allow to cool for 15 min.

Beat the butter and sugar in a separate bowl, then gradually add the eggs.

Sift in the flour, bicarbonate of soda and vanilla extract and stir until combined and smooth.

Pour in the date and tea mixture and combine.

Transfer the mixture to the dish and bake for 60–90 min.

Meanwhile, heat the butter, demerara and caster sugar and syrup in a small pan over a low heat, whisking continuously. Remove from the heat, and stir in the cream and vanilla essence. Return to the heat for a further 2–3 min until smooth.

Pour the sauce over the sponge and serve warm.

Cookies are made of butter and love.

NORWEGIAN PROVERB

SUSSEX POND PUDDING

When the tides are pulling you every which way, enjoy this lemon-and-sunshine-filled pudding and become as calm as a smooth Sussex pond.

Serves 6

Ingredients

···

For the pastry:
225 g/8 oz self-raising flour
110 g/4 oz shredded suet
90 ml/3 fl oz milk
60 ml/2 fl oz water

For the filling:
200 g/7 oz light brown sugar
200 g/7 oz butter, diced
2 large lemons

Preparation method

Grease a 1½ litre/53 fl oz pudding basin.

In a large bowl, sift the flour and mix in the suet.

Gradually pour in the milk and water together, stirring continuously to form a dough. Leave aside a quarter of the dough to be used later.

On a lightly floured work surface, roll out the remaining dough to form a large round. Use this to line the pudding basin.

Pour half the sugar and half the butter into the bottom of the pudding basin. Use a skewer to make several holes through the lemons. Place them in the pudding basin, then top up with the remaining butter and sugar.

Use the remaining pastry to form a round lid, pressing the edges together to seal. Place baking paper over the top of the basin and then cover with aluminium foil. Use string to secure.

Boil the basin in a large, covered pan for 3–4 hrs, topping up the water to come halfway up the basin throughout cooking.

'ELLO TREACLE TART

A cheeky confection of treacle and pastry, see a slice of this on a plate and you won't be able to resist asking if you can take it for a bite.

Serves 6–8

Ingredients

....

For the pastry:
225 g/8 oz plain flour
110 g/4 oz butter, diced
1 egg, beaten
1 tbsp cold water

For the filling:
450 g/1 lb golden syrup
75 g/3 oz fresh white breadcrumbs
pinch of ground ginger (optional)
grated zest of 1 lemon
juice of ½ lemon

Preparation method

In a large bowl, sift the flour and add the butter, rubbing together using your fingertips. Fold in the egg to form a dough, adding water if necessary.

On a lightly floured work surface, knead the dough until smooth.

Line a 23 cm/9 in tart tin with the dough, prick the base with a fork, and chill in the fridge for 30 min.

Preheat the oven to 190 °C/375 °F/Gas 5.

Line the pastry with baking paper, fill with baking beans, and bake for 15 min. Remove the baking paper and beans and return to the oven for a further 5 min, or until golden brown.

In a large bowl, combine the syrup, breadcrumbs, ginger, lemon zest and juice, then pour into the pastry case. Bake for 30 min.

By the way, we never eat anyone's health, always drink it. Why should we not stand up now and then and eat a tart to somebody's success?

JEROME K. JEROME

The Queen of Hearts,
she made some tarts,
All on a summer's day,
The Knave of Hearts,
he stole those tarts,
And took them clean away!

ANONYMOUS

VANILLABERRY CHESECAKE

Relax into the smooth creaminess of the vanilla cheesecake and wake up your senses with the kick of sharp blackberry. More reviving than a nap any day!

Serves 6–8

Ingredients

....

For the base:
200 g/7 oz digestive biscuits
50 g/2 oz butter

For the filling:
seeds of 1 vanilla pod
500 g/1 lb 2 oz full-fat cream cheese
3 eggs, beaten
juice of ½ lemon
90 ml/3 fl oz double cream

50 g/2 oz plain flour
200 g/7 oz caster sugar

For the blackberry purée:
110 g/4 oz blackberries
2 tsp caster sugar

Preparation method

Preheat the oven to 130 °C/250 °F/Gas 1. Grease a
20 cm/8 in. easy-release or springform cake tin and line
with baking paper.

Grind the digestive biscuits until they resemble
breadcrumbs. Gently heat the butter until melted, then
mix in with the biscuits. Transfer the mixture into the cake
tin, and press down with the bottom of a glass to compact
and even it out. Chill in the fridge for 30 min.

To make the cheesecake filling, beat the vanilla seeds and
cream cheese in a large bowl until combined, then add
the eggs, lemon juice and cream. Stir well. Add the flour
and sugar, and continue to stir until smooth.

Transfer to the cake tin.

To make the purée, gently heat the blackberries and sugar until the sugar is melted and the berries soften. Use a blender to form a smooth purée, straining if necessary, then pour this on top of the cheesecake.

Bake for 40 min, then allow to cool completely before removing from the tin.

Too many cooks, in baking
rock cakes, get misled by
the word 'rock'.

P. G. WODEHOUSE

AUTUMN CRUMBLE

When the air grows sharp and red leaves tumble, you
know it's time for autumn crumble! Use the turn in
the weather as an excuse to tuck into this apple and
blackberry treat.

Serves 4

Ingredients

....

For the filling:
25 g/1 oz butter
3 cooking apples, peeled, cored and sliced
150 g/5 oz caster sugar
75 g/3 oz fresh blackberries

For the crumble:
110 g/4 oz plain flour
50 g/2 oz butter, diced
50 g/2 oz caster sugar

Preparation method

Preheat the oven to 180 °C/350 °F/Gas 4.

Gently heat the butter in a small pan until melted, then add the apple slices and warm through, until they soften. Add the sugar and stir well.

Once the sugar has melted, add the blackberries and stir, then remove from the heat.

In a large bowl, sift the flour and add the butter and sugar. Use your fingertips to rub together to create a coarse, breadcrumb texture.

Transfer the filling into a 23 cm/9 in. ovenproof dish. Sprinkle the crumble mixture on top of the filling, making sure you leave no gaps around the sides.

Bake for 20 min, or until golden brown.

HAPPY PIE

Who can resist a smile when taking a bite of happy pie? This classic pie, packed with apples, can't fail to spread cheer.

Serves 6

Ingredients

....

For the pastry:
340 g/12 oz plain flour
pinch of salt
150 g/5 oz butter
1 tbsp caster sugar
1 egg, beaten
1 tsp of water

For the filling:
700 g/1½ lb cooking apples, peeled, cored and sliced
juice of ½ lemon
110 g/4 oz sultanas

75 g/3 oz brown sugar
grated zest of 1 orange
pinch of ground cinnamon
pinch of freshly grated nutmeg
1 tbsp milk

To serve:
1 tbsp caster sugar

Preparation method

Preheat the oven to 200 °C/400 °F/Gas 6.

In a large bowl, combine the flour, salt and butter, and rub together until it resembles breadcrumbs. Add the sugar, egg and a splash of water to form a dough.

Knead on a lightly floured work surface, then roll out gently. Use two thirds of the pastry to line a 1 litre/35 fl oz pie dish.

In a bowl, sprinkle the apples with the lemon juice, then layer the apples, sultanas, sugar, orange zest, cinnamon and nutmeg in the pie dish.

Use the remaining pastry to form the pie lid, brushing the edges with milk and pressing together. Brush the top with milk, then make a slit in the centre of the pie lid to let steam escape.

Bake for 30 min, or until golden brown, then sprinkle caster sugar on top and serve.

I like a cook who smiles
out loud when he tastes
his own work.

ROBERT FARRAR CAPON

I know the look of an apple that is roasting and sizzling on the hearth on a winter's evening, and know the comfort that comes of eating it hot.

MARK TWAIN

Of all the several kinds
of sumptuous fare,
There's none that can
with Apple-pye compare,
For costly flavour,
Or substantial paste,
For outward beauty,
Or for inward taste.

LEONARD WELSTED

DELICIOUS DISHES

TERRIFIC MR TOAD IN THE HOLE

Take a hop and a leap back to the good old days with this heart- and stomach-warming classic dish. Shiny green motorcar not included.

Serves 4

Ingredients

....

For the hole:
110 g/4 oz plain flour
pinch of salt
1 egg
300 ml/10 fl oz milk

For the toad:
15 g/½ oz butter
500 g/1 lb pork sausages

Preparation method

To make the batter, mix the flour and salt, then sift into a bowl. Beat in the egg and gradually add enough milk to form a stiff batter. Leave for 10 min. Then while stirring constantly, add in the remaining milk.

Preheat the oven to 220 °C/425 °F/Gas 7. Melt the butter in a heatproof baking dish and add the sausages. Put the dish into the oven and cook the sausages for 10 min, or until evenly browned.

Reduce the oven temperature to 180 °C/350 °F/Gas 4, pour over the batter and bake for 30 min, or until the batter is golden brown and risen.

MAMA'S BASIC PIZZA DOUGH

The pizza base is a blank canvas, ready for your mouthwateringly tasty cooking creativity. Master this recipe and become the Botticelli of pizza base cooks.

Serves 4

Ingredients

....

½ tsp sugar
25 g/1 oz yeast
150 ml/5 fl oz tepid water
450 g/1 lb plain flour
1 tsp salt
1 tbsp olive oil

Preparation method

Mix the sugar, yeast and 2 tbsp of the tepid water to a paste. Cover with a damp cloth and set aside in a warm place for 15 min or until the mixture is frothy.

Mix the flour and salt and sift into a large warmed bowl. Add the remaining tepid water and oil and the yeast mixture, and mix to a smooth dough. Knead for about 8 min or until smooth and elastic.

Set aside in a warm place for 45 min or until the dough has doubled in size. The dough is now ready to use.

FUNKY CHICKEN PIE

Don't get mad, get funky! This creamy chicken pie is smooth on the tongue with an electric lemon-and-herb background flavour, giving your day the kick it needs.

Serves 4–6

Ingredients

50 g/2 oz butter
110 g/4 oz sliced mushrooms
25 g/1 oz flour
300 ml/10 fl oz milk
275 g/10 oz cooked chicken, chopped
175 g/6 oz cooked ham, chopped
½ tsp ground mace
1 tsp dried mixed herbs
salt and pepper
juice of ½ lemon

225 g/8 oz rough puff pastry
1 egg, beaten with a little milk

Preparation method

Preheat the oven to 190 °C/375 °F/Gas 5.

Melt 25 g/1 oz of butter in a saucepan. Add the mushrooms and fry for 3 min. Transfer to a plate.

Melt the other half of the butter in the pan. Stir in the flour to form a smooth paste. Stirring constantly, slowly add the milk and bring to the boil. Add the remaining ingredients. Cook for 3–5 min.

Transfer to a deep, medium-sized pie dish.

Roll out the pastry until it is about 7.5 mm/¼ in. thick. Cover the pie dish with the pastry, trimming the ends to fit. Brush with the egg mixture.

Bake for 30–35 min or until the pastry is deep golden brown.

GOODE SHEPHERD'S PIE

Put on your fluffiest wool jumper and let this pie guide you through the long nights with warmth and hearty good cheer.

Serves 4–6

Ingredients

....

675 g/1½ lb potatoes
2 tbsp cooking oil
1 onion, chopped
110 g/4 oz mushrooms, sliced
575 g/1¼ lb cooked lamb, minced
3 tbsp tomato purée
½ tsp dry mustard
salt and pepper
150 ml/5 fl oz well-seasoned gravy
25 g/1 oz butter

Preparation method

Preheat the oven to 180 °C/350 °F/Gas 4.

Cook the potatoes in boiling, salted water for 15–20 min.

Heat the oil in a saucepan. Add the onion and mushrooms and fry for 5 min.

Stir in the lamb, tomato purée, mustard, salt and pepper to taste. Pour over the gravy and bring to the boil. Then simmer for 5 min and transfer to a pie dish.

Drain the potatoes, then mash them with the butter and add salt and pepper to taste. Spoon the mixture into the dish and put in the oven.

Bake for 20–25 min, or until the potatoes are browned.

COSY COTTAGE PIE

This pie tastes like being curled up on the hearth in the warm glow of the fireplace and is essential for the days when the wind is rattling at the windows.

Serves 4

Ingredients

1 tbsp oil
1 onion, chopped
340 g/12 oz cooked beef, minced
2 tomatoes, peeled and chopped
2 tsp Worcester sauce
1 tbsp tomato chutney
1 tsp tarragon vinegar
1 tbsp chopped thyme
1 tbsp plain flour
425 ml/¾ pint beef stock gravy
browning (optional)

450 g/1 lb mashed potatoes
(See Goode Shepherd's Pie for instructions)
25 g/1 oz butter

Preparation method

Preheat the oven to 200 °C/400 °F/Gas 6.

Heat the oil in a frying pan and gently cook the onion; allow to brown slightly.

Add the beef, tomatoes, Worcestershire sauce, tomato chutney, vinegar and thyme. Sprinkle with the flour and stir into the meat. Cook over a low heat for 2 min.

Stirring continuously, add the stock and bring to the boil. Simmer for 20 min, adding more stock if necessary. Season with salt and pepper, and add some gravy browning if required.

Tip into a pie dish and leave for a few minutes until slightly cooled.

Spread the mashed potato on the top. Fork it up to leave the surface rough or draw the fork over the surface to mark with a pattern.

Dot the top with butter.

Place the pie on a baking sheet in the oven for 20–30 min, or until the potato is golden brown and crisp.

'Tis an ill cook that cannot lick his own fingers.

WILLIAM SHAKESPEARE

What I say is that, if a man really likes potatoes, he must be a pretty decent sort of fellow.

A. A. MILNE

After a good dinner one can forgive anybody, even one's own relations.

OSCAR WILDE

MERMAID'S PIE

When the seas are raging and you've battled too many sea monsters, Mermaid's Pie is the magical remedy to rejuvenate your day.

Serves 6

Ingredients

900 g/2 lb fillet haddock, whiting, cod or a mixture of any of them
425 ml/¾ pint milk
½ onion, sliced
6 peppercorns
1 bay leaf
salt and pepper
5 hardboiled eggs, quartered
1 tbsp chopped parsley
25 g/1 oz butter

25/1 oz plain flour
2 tbsp cream
675 g/1½ lb mashed potatoes (see
Goode Shepherd's Pie for instructions)

Preparation method

Preheat the oven to 180 °C/350 °F/Gas 4.

Lay the fish fillets in a roasting pan.

Heat the milk with the onion, peppercorns, bay leaf and a
pinch of salt.

Pour over the fish and cook in the oven for about 15 min,
until the fish is firm and creamy looking.

Strain off the milk, reserving it for the sauce. Flake the
fish into a pie dish and add the eggs. Sprinkle over the
parsley.

Heat the butter in a saucepan, stir in the flour and cook
for 1 minute. Draw off the heat and gradually add the
reserved milk.

Return to the heat and stir, bringing slowly to the boil. Taste and add salt and pepper as needed. Stir in the cream and pour over the fish, mixing it with a palette knife or spoon.

Spread a layer of mashed potatoes on the top and mark with a fork in a criss-cross pattern. Dot with butter.

Place on a baking sheet and brown in the oven for about 10 min.

I don't think a really good pie can be made without a dozen or so children peeking over your shoulder as you stoop to look in at it every little while.

JOHN GOULD

YES WE FLAN!

A cheery leek and bacon flan with an upbeat of mustard to pick you up and put pep in your step.

Serves 4

Ingredients

··

Ready-made shortcrust pastry

For the filling:
15 g/½ oz butter
white of 5 small or 3 large leeks, washed and finely chopped
55 g/2 oz bacon, de-rinded and chopped
2 egg yolks
150 ml/5 fl oz double cream
salt and pepper
good-quality coarse-grain mustard
fresh Parmesan cheese, grated

Preparation method

Roll out the pastry and line a 20 cm/8 in. flan ring. Leave in the refrigerator to relax for 30 min.

Preheat the oven to 190 °C/375 °F/Gas 5.

Bake the pastry case blind. Remove from the oven and turn it down to 170 °C/325 °F/Gas 3.

Melt the butter and cook the leeks until fairly soft. In a second pan fry the bacon, in its own fat, until it begins to brown. Drain well on absorbent paper.

Mix together the egg yolks and cream. Add the leeks and bacon. Season with salt and pepper.

Spread a fairly thick layer of mustard on the base of the flan and then pour in the filling. Sprinkle evenly with Parmesan.

Bake for 30 min or until the filling is set and golden brown.

BIG BEEF BOURGUIGNON

A slow cook but fast pick-me-up. Linger in the kitchen while this dish bakes and let your senses bathe in the warmth and aroma.

Serves 6

Ingredients

2 tbsp oil
225 g/8 oz smoked bacon, sliced into strips
675 g/1½ lb steak, cubed
1 tbsp plain flour
300 ml/10 fl oz beef stock
150 ml/5 fl oz red wine
1 bay leaf
½ tsp dried mixed herbs
1 tbsp chopped fresh parsley
salt and pepper

110 g/4 oz small pickling onions
110 g/4 oz button mushrooms

Preparation method

Preheat the oven to 170 °C/325 °F/Gas 3.

Heat the oil in a frying pan. Add the bacon and fry for 5 min, or until it is evenly browned. Drain on kitchen towels and transfer to a large ovenproof dish.

Add the beef to the pan and fry for 5–8 min, or until it is evenly browned. Add to the bacon.

Pour off all but 2 tbsp of the fat and stir in the flour to form a smooth paste.

Gradually stir in the stock and wine, and bring to the boil. Simmer for 5 min, stirring constantly, or until the liquid has thickened.

Add the bay leaf, herbs, parsley and salt and pepper to taste, and pour over the meat.

Cover the dish and put into the oven. Cook for 1½ hrs. Add the onions and mushrooms to the casserole and cook for a further hour, or until the meat is cooked through and tender.

Cooking is at once a
child's play and adult joy.
And cooking done with care
is an act of love.

CRAIG CLAIRBORNE

RIBS TO SPARE

Some days you have love and humour and ribs to spare; invite round friends and family for sticky fingers and smiles.

Serves 8

Ingredients

....

2.5 kg/5 lb skinned pork belly pieces (American spare ribs)

For the marinade:
4 tbsp runny honey
4 tbsp soy sauce
1 garlic clove, crushed
juice of 2 lemons
salt and pepper

Preparation method

Mix together the ingredients for the marinade and soak the spare ribs in it for at least 1 hr. The longer they marinate the better.

Preheat the oven to 180 °C/350 °F/Gas 4.

Put the ribs, with the marinade, into a roasting pan and bake, basting occasionally, for 1½ hrs.

*One cannot think well,
love well, sleep well, if one
has not dined well.*

VIRGINIA WOOLF

After a full belly all is poetry.

FRANK McCOURT

CLOUDY DAY CHEESE SOUFFLÉ

Are there thunderclouds on the horizon? Bring a ray of sunshine into your life with this cheesy, airy dinner.

Serves 4

Ingredients

....

25 g/1 oz butter
25 g/1 oz plain flour
150 ml/5 fl oz milk
salt and pepper
3 egg yolks
75 g/3 oz cheese, grated
3 egg whites, stiffly beaten

Preparation method

Preheat oven to 200 °C/400 °F/Gas 6.

Melt the butter in a saucepan and stir in the flour to form a smooth paste.

Gradually stir in the milk and bring to the boil. Cook for 2–3 min, stirring constantly, or until the mixture thickens. Season with salt and pepper to taste.

Remove from the heat and stir in the egg yolks and cheese. Fold in the egg whites and spoon into a greased soufflé dish. Bake for 30 min, or until the soufflé has risen and is golden brown.

A POT A RICOTTA

What's better than a hug in a mug? A pot a ricotta!
Embrace your taste buds and your stomach with this rich
and cheesy dish.

Serves 4

Ingredients

....

840 g/1¾ lb ricotta cheese
4 egg yolks
1 egg
175 g/6 oz fresh Parmesan cheese, grated
50 g/2 oz unsalted butter, softened
salt and freshly ground black pepper
grated nutmeg

To serve:
pesto sauce

Preparation method

Preheat the oven to 190 °C/375 °F/Gas 5.

Mix together the ricotta, egg yolks, egg, Parmesan cheese and butter. Beat well and season to taste with salt, pepper and nutmeg.

Turn into a buttered 1 litre/35 fl oz ovenproof dish.

Bake for 30 min. Cool slightly. Turn out onto a plate. Spread with the pesto sauce, or dilute pesto with oil depending on your preference and serve while still warm.

NUTS ABOUT CRUMBLE

Go crazy for this savoury, wintry crumble that starts as a stew but takes a sharp left turn at crumble. A little bit odd but a whole lotta good.

Serves 4

Ingredients

900 g/2 lb fresh chestnuts (if not available, use whole tinned chestnuts)
2 celery sticks, chopped
1 carrot, peeled and chopped
white part of 2 leeks, chopped
425 ml/¾ pint white or vegetable stock
freshly ground black pepper

For the topping:

3 slices wholemeal bread made into crumbs
1 large carrot, peeled and grated
1 tbsp finely chopped fresh mint

Preparation method

Preheat the oven to 200 °C/400 °F/Gas 6.

Make a slit in the skin of each chestnut and place in a large pan of cold water. Bring to the boil and cook slowly for 20 min. Remove from the water and peel. If the chestnuts become difficult to peel, return to hot water for a few minutes to reheat, as chestnuts are easier to peel when warm.

While the chestnuts are cooking, lightly boil the celery, leeks and whole carrot in the stock until they are just tender.

Mix together the chestnuts, vegetables and stock. Season well with pepper and pile into a pie dish.

Mix the breadcrumbs, remaining grated carrot and chopped mint, and sprinkle it over the chestnut pie.

Bake for 20 min.

*A good meal soothes the soul
as it regenerates the body.*

FREDERICK W. HACKWOOD

When someone asks if you'd like cake or pie, why not say you want cake and pie?

LISA LOEB

THE WHOLE ENCHILADA

Some days you need the big shebang, the entire 9 yards, the whole enchilada! How else to do this than with these delicious, spicy enchiladas?

Serves 6

Ingredients

12 corn tortillas
16 oz mozzarella or queso blanco
12 oz/350 g chicken or Quorn pieces

For the sauce:
1 tbsp olive oil
2 cloves garlic, minced
½ onion, minced
2½ tsp chilli powder
½ tsp dried basil
⅛ tsp freshly ground black pepper

⅛ tsp salt
¼ tsp ground cumin
1 tsp dried parsley
4 tbsp tomato salsa
175 g/6 oz passata
350 ml/12 fl oz water
2–3 tbsp oil

Preparation method

Preheat the oven to 180 °F/350 °C/Gas 4.

Sauté the garlic in the oil for 1–2 min.

Stir in the onion, chilli powder, basil, pepper, salt, cumin, parsley, salsa and passata, then add the water and bring to the boil. Reduce the heat and simmer for 15–20 min.

Fry the chicken or Quorn on either side until cooked. Mix half the sauce and half the cheese in with the chicken or Quorn.

Wrap the chicken or Quorn in individual tortillas and place in an ovenproof dish.

Pour the remaining sauce and cheese over the top and bake for 15 min.

The smell of good bread baking, like the sound of lightly flowing water, is indescribable in its evocation of innocence and delight.

M. F. K. FISHER

We light the oven so that everyone may bake bread in it.

JOSÉ MARTÍ

SAVOURY BAKES

BAKER'S OWN BREAD

There are some smells guaranteed to lift your spirits – just-mown grass, laundry on the line and freshly baked bread. Make your nose smile with this classic recipe.

Serves 4

Ingredients

23 ml/1½ tbsp sugar
15 g/½ oz yeast
475 ml/16 fl oz tepid water
675 g/1½ lb plain flour
10 ml/2 tsp salt

Preparation method

Mix the yeast, 7.5 ml/1½ tsp of the sugar and 30 ml/ 2 tbsp of the water into a paste. Put in a warm place for 15 min, until the mixture appears frothy. Mix the flour and salt and sift into a large bowl. Add the yeast mixture, the remaining water and sugar, and mix to a smooth dough. Knead until elastic and smooth, which should take about 10 min. Put in a warm place until the dough has doubled in size, which should take roughly 1–1¼ hrs.

Preheat oven to 230 °C/450 °F/Gas 8.

Take the dough out and knead again for 8 min. Shape into a loaf and put into a well-greased 1 kg/2 lb loaf tin. Put in a warm place for 30 min or until the dough has risen to the top of the tin.

Put the tin into the oven for 15 min. Reduce the oven temperature to 220 °C/425 °F/Gas 7 and continue to bake for 30 min. The bread is cooked if it sounds hollow when knocked on the bottom with your knuckle. Cool on a wire rack.

WHOLESOME
HEART BREAD

Nurture your heart and soul with this wholesome, honeyed bread.

Serves 4

Ingredients

....

23 ml/1 ½ tbsp sugar
15 g/½ oz yeast
475 ml/16 fl oz tepid water
675 g/1 ½ lb wholewheat flour
10 ml/2 tsp salt
15 ml/1 tbsp clear honey

Preparation method

Mix the yeast, 7.5 ml/1½ tsp of the sugar and 30 ml/ 2 tbsp of the water into a paste. Cover with a damp tea towel and put in a warm place for 15 min or until the mixture is frothy. Warm a large bowl and mix the flour and salt in it. Add the yeast mixture, the remaining sugar, water and the honey, mixing until the contents resemble a smooth dough. Knead for 10 min, creating a smooth and elastic dough. Put in a warm place until the dough has doubled in size, which should take about 1–1½ hrs.

Preheat the oven to 230 °C/450 °F/Gas 8.

Take out of the warm place and knead the dough for a further 8 min. Grease a 1 kg/2 lb loaf tin. Roughly shape the dough into a loaf and place in the tin. Put in a warm place for approximately 30 min, until the dough has risen to the top of the tin.

Bake for 15 min, then reduce the oven temperature to 220 °C/425 °F/Gas 7 and bake for a further 30 min. Cool on a wire rack.

FIZZY FEELINGS SODA BREAD

When you want fast food with a delicious taste, simply grab a soda. Bicarbonate of soda, that is, and make this quick and simple bread.

Serves 4

Ingredients

....

1 kg/2 lb flour
10 ml/2 tsp
bicarbonate of soda
10 ml/2 tsp salt
350 ml/12 fl oz buttermilk

Preparation method

Preheat the oven to 220 °C/425 °F/Gas 7.

Warm a large bowl. Mix the flour, bicarbonate of soda and salt, and sift into the warmed bowl.

Make a well in the bowl and add the buttermilk, stirring until the dough is smooth. Shape it into a large deep circle.

Transfer to a well-greased baking sheet, then cut a deep cross in the centre.

Put the baking sheet into the oven and bake for 35 min or until the top is golden brown.

Cool on a wire rack.

*I feel a recipe is only
a theme, which an intelligent
cook can play each time
with a variation.*

JEHANE BENOÎT

When I cannot write a
poem, I bake biscuits and
feel just as pleased.

ANNE MORROW LINDBERGH

SUMMER BREAD

Whether the sun is shining or not, this Italian bread tastes like warm evenings outside and is perfect for any hearty summer spread.

Serves 4

Ingredients

30 g/1 oz fresh yeast
225 ml/8 fl oz warm water
450 g/1 lb strong plain flour
10 ml/2 tsp salt
30 ml/2 tbsp olive oil

For a herb Summer Bread:
1 tbsp basil
1 tsp onion powder
1 tsp garlic powder
1 tsp oregano

Preparation method

Stir the yeast into the warm water until it dissolves.

Sift the flour and salt onto a work surface, and make a well in the centre. Pour in the dissolved yeast and olive oil. Gradually mix in the flour and, if baking the herb summer bread, add in the remaining ingredients, and when well mixed, knead the dough for 8 min.

Put the dough in a lightly floured bowl. Cover with a damp tea towel and leave to rise in a warm place. This will take about 1 hr.

Preheat the oven to 230 °C/450 °F or Gas 8.

Mould into a loaf shape and set aside in a warm place until it's 1½ times its original size. Bake for 10 min.

Reduce the heat to 190 °C/375 °F/Gas 5 and bake for a further 45 min. Remove to a cooling rack and let cool before eating.

HAPPY SNAPPY BREADS

When you're feeling angry, don't start smashing plates, start snapping breads! Enjoy this light, crisp bread and your worries will be gone in a snap.

Serves 4

Ingredients

400 g/14 oz rye flour
1 tsp sea salt, ground
10 g/⅓ oz fresh yeast
350 ml/12 fl oz water, tepid

Preparation method

Preheat the oven to 200 °C/400 °F/Gas 6.

Mix the flour and salt in a large bowl. Disintegrate the yeast into the tepid water, and whisk until the yeast is dissolved and the water is milky.

Add the yeast mixture to the flour and stir. The result should be a sticky, stiff paste. Cover the bowl with a damp tea towel and set aside in a warm place for 1 hr, or until slightly risen. Line two baking sheets with baking parchment.

Divide the dough into 12 balls and roll each section out into a disc approximately the size of a small plate. Using a skewer, pierce the surface of the dough all over with holes.

Place a disc on each tray and bake for 15–18 min until the bread is hard and crisp. Repeat with the remaining dough. Remove to a cooling rack and let cool before eating.

CHEESE WHIRLWINDS

Take your taste buds for a whirl with these peppery twists, guaranteed to put a big cheesy smile on your face.

Makes 50

Ingredients

....

170 g/6 oz plain flour
pinch of salt
100 g/3½ oz butter
45 g/1½ oz grated Parmesan or mixed Parmesan and Gruyère or Cheddar cheese
pinch of pepper
pinch of cayenne pepper
pinch of dry English mustard
1 egg, beaten

Preparation method

Preheat the oven to 190 °C/375 °F/Gas 5.

Mix the salt and flour and sift into a large bowl. With your fingers, rub the butter into the flour until the mixture resembles fine breadcrumbs. Add in the cheese and seasonings to taste.

Add in the egg a little at a time until the mixture is bound and resembles a stiff dough. Set aside in the fridge for 10 min.

Line a baking sheet with greaseproof paper. Roll the dough into a large rectangle and cut into 9 x 2 cm/ 3½ x ¾ in. strips, roughly 3 mm deep. Twist each strip 3–4 times.

Bake for 8–10 min or until biscuit brown.

Cookery is become an art,
a noble science: cooks
are gentlemen.

ROBERT BURTON

Cooking is like love. It should be entered into with abandon or not at all.

HARRIET VAN HORNE

JOLLY GOOD MUFFINS

It will be hard to smile around your stiff upper lip but these English muffins will put you in such a jolly mood you won't be able to resist trying.

Ingredients

5 ml/1 tsp sugar
15 g/½ oz yeast
75 ml/3 fl oz tepid water
450 g/1 lb flour
pinch of salt
150 ml/5 fl oz tepid milk
1 egg, beaten
25 g/1 oz butter, melted

Preparation method

Mix the sugar, yeast and water until it is a sticky paste. Cover with a damp tea towel and set aside in a warm place until frothy, which should take roughly 15 min. Warm a large bowl. Mix the flour and salt, and sift into the bowl. Make a well and add the yeast paste, egg, milk and butter, and mix until a dough. Knead until smooth and elastic, which should take about 15 min. Put in a warm place until the dough is twice the size.

Preheat the oven to 230 °C/450 °F/Gas 8.

Take the dough out and knead for 3 min. Roll out the dough into a rough circle about 1.25 cm/½ in. thick, then cut into circles with a 10 cm/4 in. circumference pastry cutter. Grease a baking sheet and lightly flour, then transfer the circles. Put in a warm place for 20 min or until the circles have doubled in size.

Bake for 5 min, then turn over and bake for 5 min on the other side, until both sides of the muffins are golden brown.

I'M FILOS FINE

Give yourself those happy filos with these little bites of pastry, vegetables, herbs and joy.

Serves 4

Ingredients
....

3 sheets filo pastry
1 small aubergine, finely sliced into semicircles
2 small courgettes, finely sliced into semicircles
3 small tomatoes, finely sliced, de-seeded and cut into semicircles
60 ml/4 tbsp olive oil
5 ml/1 tsp fresh thyme leaves
5 ml/1 tsp fresh oregano, chopped
salt and freshly ground black pepper

Preparation method

Preheat the oven to 200 °C/400 °F/Gas 6.

Cut the filo sheets into rectangles about 7.5 cm/3 in. wide. Lightly oil the pastry and place three layers on top of each other on an oiled baking tray. Using the combination of vegetables you prefer, lay in rows on each rectangle of pastry.

Brush sparingly with olive oil and add the herbs, salt and pepper to taste. Bake for 15–20 min. Trim the sides neatly. Best served warm.

*Good food is the foundation
of genuine happiness.*

AUGUSTE ESCOFFIER

The pleasant hours of
our life are all connected
by a more or less tangible
link, with some memory
of the table.

CHARLES PIERRE MONSELET

If you're interested in finding out more about our books,
find us on Facebook at **Summersdale Publishers** and
follow us on Twitter at **@Summersdale**.

www.summersdale.com